To Tenten —
Happy Homeschooling!

Homeschool WITH Confidence

a goal-setting guide for teens

by Suki Wessling

CHATOYANT

Chatoyant
PO Box 832
Aptos, CA 95001
www.Chatoyant.com

Publisher's Cataloging in Publication Data
Wessling, Suki.
  Homeschool with Confidence: A Goal-Setting Guide for Teens / Suki Wessling.
    p. cm.
  Summary: Homeschool with Confidence helps homeschooled teens focus on what matters, organize their lives, and take ownership of their education.
  ISBN 978-0-9661452-9-8
  [1. YOUNG ADULT NONFICTION / Inspirational & Personal Growth
  2. YOUNG ADULT NONFICTION / Careers
  3. YOUNG ADULT NONFICTION / Social Topics / Self-Esteem & Self-Reliance]
Printed in the United States.
Library of Congress Control Number: 2017904017

Dedicated to my students—past, present, and future—and to my children. Each one of you has taught me much more than you know!

Thanks to the Fall, 2016 Athena's students who agreed to let me use their words in this book.

☺ Table of Contents ⇐

Introduction

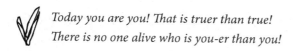

Today you are you! That is truer than true!
There is no one alive who is you-er than you!

–Dr. Seuss

Do you need this book?

This is a book for homeschooled kids. I think it's best for teens, but if you are younger you can decide if you're ready for it.

This is not a book for homeschooling parents. I give your parent permission to read along and support you as you use this book, but this book is really for you.

Why?

Because homeschoolers have a problem that schoolers don't have.

You're not a sheep

Have you ever heard of "herd mentality"? This is part of how the human brain works. We may be very independent thinkers in normal life, but as soon as we're part of a group of people who are all doing the same thing, we seem to turn off our independent brains (to a certain extent) and follow along.

So schoolers have it easy in a way: When they're in ninth grade and the school tells them to take a math class, they take the math class that appears on their schedule. That's pretty darn easy. It's what everyone else is doing.

Herd mentality, right?

Homeschoolers don't have much of a herd. Even though there are more and more of us each year, we're all doing different things. We don't move in packs from one classroom to the next. We are the ultimate independent thinkers in the kid community.

But that means we have a lot more decisions to make than schoolers do. We can't just go with the pack; we have to figure out what's right for us and figure out how to make it happen.

Why did I write this book?

I'm going to tell you a secret about me: Before I had kids, I never knew that I could set a goal and achieve it.

You're thinking I must be pretty lame, but I was considered pretty successful. I dropped out of high school (that's the homeschooler in me) but graduated from Stanford University. I got a graduate degree and became a college instructor. I left my teaching job when I moved to be with my husband, so I started a graphic design business. I taught myself how to build websites. Then I started a publishing business.

Then I had kids, and I helped their schools improve their Web presence and communications.

In all this time, I never once thought about what I wanted to do, figured out the path to get there, took the various steps I needed to take, and then achieved the thing I wanted to do.

In other words, I never set a goal.

No one had ever pointed out to me that setting and achieving goals is what leads to people feeling happy and satisfied in their lives.

Wait, is this a book about goal-setting (*BO*-ring) or happiness?

Well, it's actually both. Studies have found that people who learn to set goals and strive for them are not only more successful in the usual ways we think about success: money, good jobs, a nice house, a family. People who learn to set goals and strive for them are actually happier and *feel* more successful…even when they don't achieve their goals.

My dissatisfaction ☹

I have to admit that I spent a lot of time before I had children feeling this sort of low-level dissatisfaction with everything I was doing. None of it seemed to *get me anywhere*.

But that was simply because I didn't know where I wanted to go.

Goal-setting ≠ Success

You might think that this book is about how to win prizes, make lots of money, and get featured on the covers of magazines.

It's not.

Goal-setting is about thinking about what you want and who you are

Goal-setting is about learning what's important and what's not

Goal-setting is about learning to challenge yourself

Goal-setting is about learning to forgive yourself

Goal-setting is about learning to achieve goals

Goal-setting is about figuring out how to change your goals

Goal-setting is sometimes about learning from failure

Goal-setting is always about experiencing success

Why use this book?

You are probably reading this book because a parent or teacher told you to. In fact, my children and students are reading this book because I told them to!

But in order to use this book well—to "achieve success" with this book—you need to use it for *you*.

Yep, I'm asking you to be totally selfish in your desire to get the most from this book.

As a homeschooler, your education is yours and yours alone. Everything you do has to be part of what you want to get from life.

It's true for all of us: some of what we want to get from life is to get other people (parents, employers, neighbors, etc.) to stop nagging us. This is a totally awesome goal for some things in life. You want to have a happy home life, and if part of that is emptying the dishwasher every morning, well then, darn it, that can be a personal goal. (Even when the person who came up with the idea for the goal is your parent.)

But what's more important is that most things you do at this point in your life are for you and your future life alone. Once you are on your own and pursuing a career, it's not for your parent, the rest of your family, your friends, your neighbors… It's for you.

And if you end up with a job you don't love, it will be up to you to fix it.

Meeting your goals starts now

Since this is the life you are aiming for, you might as well lay the foundations right now.

Remember herd behavior? You can't depend on it. You are a homeschooler with an independent mind. It's your job to develop that mind to achieve the goals you want to achieve.

I hope this book will help you do that.

How to use this book

Of course, you can use this book any way you'd like. It might end up being a convenient coaster for your tea. However, here's what I would suggest: Set aside at least 6 weeks to use this book, one chapter per week. Try to plan not to take more than 10 weeks or you'll lose momentum. Only take fewer than 6 weeks if you really are doing all the exercises and feel like you are taking the time to digest what's in each chapter before you move on.

OK, that's my suggestion. But I trust that you're doing to do what's best for you!

A note about parents and pronouns

I am a bit of a stickler for grammar, but you might notice something already. When I refer to the adult who is your primary homeschooler, I will call "them" your "parent." That person may be singular, or it may be two people. They may be your biological parents, or they may be a responsible adult in your life. By using the singular parent but the plural "they," I'm leaving things blank for you to fill in. Parent or not, singular or not, of whatever gender they might be, in this book they will be referred to as your "parent."

Ask them to read this

A note to parents

OK, I give you permission to read this book, too.

I've come to realize that goal-setting is one of the most important skills we homeschoolers can give to our kids. There are two reasons.

First, once your children become teens, they're going to want to do things for themselves. They're going to want to have some control over what they study and how they learn. And this is great—their education *is* for them. But without set goals, homeschooling with teens can very quickly devolve into power struggles. The teens think their parent is imposing unreasonable demands on them, but can't explain why they're unreasonable. The parent knows that they're doing what's best for their kids, but can't explain why.

The second reason goal-setting is important is that, as I explained to your teen, homeschooling doesn't set implicit goals the way schooling does. Our students have choice over everything, which is not always the easiest thing. When they learn to set goals, they learn to narrow the field of possible choices to a more workable size. When they learn to change goals, they learn that when you eliminate a choice that doesn't fit your current goals, it's still there for you as an option if you realign your goals.

In my own homeschooling life, I have found goal-setting to be supremely important. When my older child was 13, I realized that we were spending more and more time arguing about why he had to do some task, or why he was even studying math at all, or why I cared that he could write a coherent argument. Of course, it's completely developmentally appropriate for your teen to argue—your teen is learning to define his or her own self, which is a pretty big and scary job. Arguing with parents is not only appropriate but healthy.

Goal-setting allowed us to focus on what our son wanted while trying to guide him in his educational choices. He and I gritted our teeth and made it through a goal-setting curriculum written for school kids. We were both relieved when it was done. But although we didn't enjoy the curriculum terribly much, the result was fantastic. Now we could talk about that task he didn't want to do, that subject he didn't want to study, or that skill he didn't want to work on in terms of his goals, not his parents' goals.

As of this writing, my older child is now 17 and applying to college. He set goals, attained a few, and changed some. He's not applying to college in exactly the same field he thought he would when he was 13, and he's also broadened his ideas of which colleges might suit his needs. We still argue about all sorts of things (he is 17, you know), but I feel that our arguments usually resolve into positive growth in our family.

My younger child is now 13, the age when I did goal-setting with my first. And boy, you couldn't find a child more different than his brother. He and I also have power struggles, arguments over what he should study, and pushback about all sorts of things. But he has completely different interests from his brother.

And now I'm faced with putting my money where my mouth is, so to speak. I am writing this book intentionally to jump-start our fall goal-setting. Because of the sort of person my younger child is, I decided to hold my goal-setting seminar at Athena's Advanced Academy, where I teach. I think having a community of kids to work on goal-setting with will be a more positive experience in this case than sitting at the kitchen table and butting heads.

For that reason, I highly recommend that if you butt heads with your teen a lot, you put together a goal-setting group to work through this book together. Group work takes the pressure off of your relationship with your child.

I hope that in four years I will be able to rewrite this note with the news that goal-setting served my second child as well as my first. But right now all I can do is assure you that from within the rather insane task of homeschooling teenagers, I feel that goal-setting has offered us a healthy, positive way to confront the choices we're faced with.

I hope that it will help you as well.

Now, hand this book back to your student, and remember that when it comes to goal-setting, you're the backup, the support person, and perhaps the schedule-keeper and chauffeur.

But only your student can drive the vehicle that is their education.

Onward!

CHAPTER 1

What are goals and why do we make them?

It is not enough to take steps which may some day lead to a goal; each step must be itself a goal and a step likewise.

–Johann Wolfgang von Goethe

Exercise: Goal-setting questionnaire

Before you read any of this book, copy and fill out the following questionnaire. Try to answer as truthfully as possible. Don't worry if your answer is "I don't know"! You can download a pretty version at SukiWessling.com/goal/.

You'll revisit this questionnaire at the end of the book, so make sure to keep it around. However, this is very important: Don't look at your completed questionnaire again until I ask you to! Yes, I have a reason for this, but I'm not going to tell you right now. Just be assured that there is a method to my madness!

What is a goal?

_____

Name a goal you met today

_____

Name a goal you haven't met

_____

How do you think your life would be better if you met more of your goals?

_____

Who could help you meet your goals?

_____

What is the difference between a dream and a goal?

_____

What is success?

_____

What is failure?

_____

Rate yourself on this table on a scale of 1 to 5 for each quality. 1 means "I am not at all like this in any way" and 5 means "This describes me really well."

I like to have an idea of what's going to happen when I get up in the morning	
I love surprises	
I like to know how things work	
I enjoy keeping things mysterious	
I like to make things from scratch	
I like to make things, but only with directions and pre-made pieces	
I like to learn about something before I experience it	
I would rather learn details after an experience	
I just want experiences and really don't like thinking about them later	
I'm the person in a group who gets ideas and leads	
I'm the person in the group who tends to stay quiet and do what others want	
I think I have a lot of control over what happens in my life	
I feel like everyone else is in charge	
If there are too many steps to follow, I get discouraged from doing something	
I like planning things out from beginning to end	
I like asking questions and learning new things	
I feel confident about things I know I'm good at	

Thanks for filling this out! If you are using a printout or photocopy, remember to stow it somewhere safe so you can access it when you get to Chapter 6.

Now: *onward* to learn about goals!

We make goals all the time

I don't know if reading this book is your idea. If you are at all like my kids, you're reading this book because your parent told you to. That's not a bad reason, actually. Adults have lots of wisdom to share, but it's typical for kids to want to figure things out for themselves.

I'm going to tell you something that will make all of this easier: This is a book about stuff you already do. Getting through this book might actually be easy, because you're going to recognize a lot of what I tell you.

So why read it?

Because sometimes we don't notice things until we really focus on them. Think of this book as another way to open your eyes to what's already happening around you.

A goal I'm working on is trying to go to bed earlier. Over the summer, I messed up my sleep schedule big time. I was getting up at noon, and going to bed at as late as 3 in the morning. Now I need to get up earlier in order to fulfill my work for every day. Last night I went to bed at 23:30 and woke up at 10, which is early for me, but I wasn't tired! I still want to get up at 8, but I'm getting closer!   Reid

You set goals all the time and you meet them all the time. I bet this morning you got out of bed. OK, one of you may be reading this book on your tablet sitting in bed, but the rest of you probably got out of bed.

Why? Well, because in order to do the rest of the things you wanted to do today, you had to get out of bed. So you set a goal—maybe it was "eat those pancakes I smell being made in the kitchen" or "get up and make pancakes"—and you did what you needed to do in order to achieve the goal—get out of bed!

Simple, right?

We all do that every day of our lives, and we do it without thinking about it. Our days are full of goals set and attained—and goals set and put off for later or abandoned entirely.

We change goals all the time

So this morning maybe you got out of bed because you knew you were going to the pool and you really love to swim. Then at breakfast the sky clouded up and then came rain, lightning, and no pool.

Oh, no. A goal postponed.

What are we going to do now? Well, we have that new board game we've been wanting to learn, but we haven't had time because we've been at the pool. Awesome! Let's learn the game.

A new goal made.

You get out the game only to see that your toddler sister found the instruction sheet, ripped it into little bits, and then chewed on them till they were slimy.

Oh, no. A goal chewed up.

But wait! We have the Internet! We can look up the rules.

A new goal made.

Just as you get your computer out, the lights go out. No Internet.

A goal shrouded in darkness.

And on and on. Our days are like this. We decide what we want to do, and we go about taking the steps that will get us there. Sometimes we have to change direction. That's goal-setting.

Can I stop reading this book now? Nope.

Avoiding "rock brain"

An educator I like made up the term "rock brain" for when you just can't let go of an idea. Most of us suffer from rock brain occasionally.

But maybe you're the most flexible kid in the world—totally, awesomely laid-back. If you truthfully answer "no" to the following three questions, you can skip to the next section:

- Do you sometimes get mad when something doesn't go as you planned it?
- Do you get annoyed at your parent when they tell you you're going to do one thing, and then something happens, and you have to change plans?
- When you can't do something exactly the way you want, do you sometimes decide not to do it at all?

That's rock brain at work. You got fixed on something—a goal—and you just can't let go of it.

The thing is, goals aren't carved into stone. People change their minds about their favorite ice cream flavors, whether they are going to take a math class online or study independently, or whether they are going to grow up to be a teacher or a geologist.

It's as important to be flexible about goals as it is to have goals in the first place. If you know you have a tendency for rock brain, it's worth keeping in mind as you work on goal-setting. It really is OK to change your mind, especially when the conditions around you change.

Why having a goal is important

In this book, I'm going to ask you to talk to other people about their goals. Often we don't think about how other people do things, but asking them can show you how others see the world. You may be surprised at how different their view is!

> Whenever I have to do something I don't think I can do, I just say no. Even if it's not that bad I end up acting like it's the worst thing ever. For example, I had to do an exercise class and it hurt and my mom said I was going to do it twice a week. After the first session I said I did not want to come back and Mom tried to tell me it was important and that I needed more exercise. But since I had to go, two days later I went back and it didn't hurt, it was just difficult. Reid

So this isn't a formal exercise, but at this point you should pause in your reading and ask someone why they think having goals is important.
[Pause here! Go ask someone why having goals is important!] ☺
Just in case no one is around to ask, I'll pretend you asked me.
My answer is that goals are important for a variety of reasons:

→ Sometimes we think we know what we want, but it's helpful to set a goal to clarify what we want and make sure we do it

→ Sometimes we have no idea what we want, so setting a goal gives us a direction to go in, so we don't just stand there doing nothing

→ Sometimes we think we're doing something useful, but when we look at our goals we realize the thing we're doing isn't useful at all

→ Having a goal helps us see that we've achieved something

→ When your parent bugs you about what you're doing, having a goal can provide a very convenient way to answer!

So why might you want to have goals? It's not necessary for you to answer that question right now—hopefully this book will help you find the answer. But maybe one of the reasons above made sense to you.

A dream is something you only think about and wish you could have or do. A goal is something (realistic) that you want and work to accomplish.,
Avery

What are short-term and long-term goals?

In this book, we're going to treat goals differently depending on whether they're short-term or long-term. Why? Because short-term goals tend to be smaller and involve fewer steps. It's easier to attain short-term goals, usually, because you don't have to invest a lot of time in them.

Long-term goals tend to be things you want to achieve on some horizon:

- It's easy to forget about them because life is full of things that get in the way of the horizon
- It's easy to get distracted from them by something else that looks enticing
- It's easy to give up on them because something else is closer, even if you don't want it as much

How to use the exercises in this book

There aren't very many chapters in this book. At the end of each chapter you'll find only a few exercises. So there aren't very many exercises in this book. It's not really a big deal to do all of them, but some of them may not speak to you. Feel free to adjust them to work better with the way you look at your life.

Some of them are called "exercises" and some are called "stretchercizes."

The **exercises** are things you can do just by looking into your own mind and living your own life. Some of you are going to be very comfortable with this, and others will find it harder. We'll discuss that in the next section.

The **stretchercizes** are going to ask you to stretch outside of your own life. Some of you are going to love this. Talking to adults? Interviewing strangers? Cool!

Others of you are going to find this a really big, uncomfortable stretch. That doesn't mean you shouldn't do it, but don't stretch so far that you're really uncomfortable. It's OK to choose adults you know well for the stretchercizes, if that makes you more comfortable. I believe that we all benefit from stretching some, but you don't have to make yourself really unhappy in the process.

What is introspection and why are some people uncomfortable with it?

This book is going to ask you to think about yourself and why you do things. That's a short description of the word "introspection." Some people love introspection—in fact, some of us who love it do it way too much and have to stop ourselves!

Others of us really feel uncomfortable with introspection—we'll do almost anything to avoid it.

If you're comfortable being introspective, skip to the next section if you'd like. If you're not, *read on*.

First, take a deep breath. Why? It's scientifically proven to be a good thing to do when you're approaching something you find uncomfortable.

Then, understand that all of us are different, and that's OK. It's actually better than OK. Imagine what the world would be like if we were all Einstein. We'd have lots of physicists and violin players, but not a single good soccer coach.

If the exercises in this book make you feel uncomfortable, or if you just feel like they're stupid and unnecessary, you're probably someone who doesn't care for introspection. However, one of the things I hope you'll get from this book is a healthier attitude toward introspection (which may be a "stretchercize" for you).

Thinking about yourself, what you're like, and what you want is the best way to be a happy, well-rounded adult. The U.S. Declaration of Independence stated that everyone has the right to pursue happiness, but some of us need a bit of a push to get on with it.

Like I said about the Stretchercizes, don't turn away from experiences just because they're hard for you or make you somewhat uncomfortable. "Get out of your comfort zone" is pretty common advice to people who feel stuck in their lives.

You're young, and you can develop the habit now not to get stuck.

Doing the exercises in this book

I think that setting students free to do things in the way that inspires them is one of the greatest things about homeschooling. So I'm not going to dictate how you do these exercises.

Here are a few suggestions—feel free to make up a different method if it works for you and your parent.

Writing

This is the traditional approach, and it's a great way to work. As a writer, I will tell you that I never really understand anything until I write it down and organize my thoughts. Also, if you are in a homeschool program that requires samples, you might find it convenient to make them this way. And furthermore, it might be one of your family's values that you do your exercises in writing, and that's fine.

But remember, all writing doesn't all have to be formal, essay-style writing. Consider being creative with your writing assignments if it's more fun for you. You can keep a journal, make comics, or write your assignments as letters to someone.

A modern-day alternative that I love is keeping a blog. You can sign up for free blog software and immediately publish your ideas for anyone to read—cool! (You can also keep your blog private and just tell certain people about it.)

Did you know learning actually <u>has to be fun</u>? When brain scientists study people learning, they find that people who are uncomfortable, unhappy, or stressed out sometimes can't learn anything at all. The people who are having fun learn the most!

Video

Video-making is a great way to organize your thoughts, too. These days, pretty much any laptop or tablet comes with the capability to make and edit videos. You can share your videos with family and friends, or post them on Youtube for anyone to see. Just make sure you feel like you're doing something useful and fun.

Discussion group

My kids and I like to form small groups to study a subject they are interested in. It's not like school, where you cram 32 people who aren't interested and 1 person who *is* interested into a room and force them to learn the same thing. A great homeschool discussion group will be made up of kids who all want to be there and contribute. This book was actually written to be used with such a group at the online school where I teach, Athena's Advanced Academy. I highly recommend this approach.

A combination of the three

The thing that makes creating stuff really fulfilling is having an audience to give you feedback. There's no reason why you can't have a discussion group that shares writing, videos, art, and more as you go through this book. I recommend it!

⏵ Exercise 1a: A goal

What is one goal (small or large) that you have set and attained yesterday or today? It should be something you don't do every day, so don't use "I got out of bed"! But it can be something pretty small if you'd like.

⏵ Exercise 1b: A failed goal

What is one goal that you did not attain recently or in the past? Do you still wish you could attain it, or have you moved on?

⏵ Stretchercize 1: Your first interview

Choose someone in your family or neighborhood. Find out one goal they have right now that they are sure they will attain today or within the week. Ask them why they came up with the goal and how they will attain it. If you like, offer to set a date to go back and make sure they attained the goal. (We'll talk about accountability later!)

⟹ Recap: In this chapter, we • • •

- • • noticed that we make goals all the time
- • • acknowledged that we change goals all the time
- • • learned to identify "rock brain"
- • • discussed why having a goal is important
- • • learned the difference between short-term and long-term goals
- • • discussed how to use the exercises in this book

- • • got introspective about introspection
- • • decided how you are going to complete the exercises

Stop here !

Wait, this chapter isn't over?

Not quite.

When I teach literature to students, I tell them that it's fine—wonderful, in fact—to devour a novel in one sitting.

I'm going to tell you the opposite. This book is not meant to be devoured. If you don't stop and do the exercises in between, you won't be able to take the steps you need to take. Especially if you are not a natural goal-setter, you might be tempted to skip doing the exercises and go on to the next chapter.

I'm asking you to stop now and go back to those exercises. Really do them so that you're prepared to get the most from the next chapter.

Onward!

CHAPTER 2
Short-term (one-step) goals

 Have a bias toward action - let's see something happen now. You can break that big plan into small steps and take the first step right away.

–Indira Gandhi

What makes a one-step goal?

I asked my mom why it's important to have goals and she said, "I think it's important to have goals because without goals it's like steering a rudderless ship—you don't really know which way you're going. Also, there is a sense of accomplishment to making and achieving a goal."

Avery

One-step goals are the sort of goals we don't even think of as goals. We just do them all the time, and it would be pretty weird if we started thinking of them as goals all the time. Imagine how bogged down you could get!

28

I have the goal of taking a step with my right foot.

Now I have the goal of taking a step with my left foot.

It would be pretty hard to get anything done! But one-step goals aren't really that simple. They're more like this:

I'm planning to make reuben sandwiches for lunch, and since we got all the ingredients yesterday at the grocery store, I can go into the kitchen right now and get started.

or

It's been raining for a week and today the sun is shining, so I'm going to take my bike out and ride around the neighborhood.

or

Taking the math pre-test is on my homeschooling checklist, and I'm sitting in front of my computer with time to spare, so I might as well do it right now.

Like I said, this is the sort of thing you do every day and don't really notice. See what I said about how most of this book is about stuff you already do?

All right: get ready to do something Right Now...

⏩ Exercise:

Do this exercise Right Now, before reading on. Do not procrastinate!

Think of something you know you are going to do today, and set it as a goal by writing it on a piece of paper, a whiteboard, or in a digital checklist. Do it and then check it off.

Right now.

I mean it.

Have you done it?

No? Go do it. Don't worry—I'll wait for you.

Yes? Read on!

Why set short-term goals?

OK, if short-term goals are so simple, why set them at all?

You probably don't remember, but at some point when you were learning to walk, an adult probably took your hands, lifted you up so you were standing on their shoes, and walked you across the room.

Why did they do such a silly thing? You probably would have learned to walk at some point anyway, right?

Well, sure, but practicing everyday activities can help us build confidence, and it can also help us build the tools we need for doing more complex things. Short-term goals are easy to set, and easy to meet. We're going to use them as a pair of adult feet to walk on—a risk-free way of learning how to build and achieve bigger goals.

If you play an instrument, you know this: you can actually change what you are able to do by practicing new skills. But there's a downside to practice: if you do it wrong, you can cement bad habits. I call this "practicing in your mistakes," and it's how pretty much all of our bad habits start. What do you do if you have a habit you don't want to have anymore? Practice the right thing! Just like a piano player might need to practice scales to learn fingering, you need to practice the steps involved in setting and meeting goals in order to learn a new skill.

Ways to document short-term goals

There are many ways to document your goals—I'm not going to tell you what the best way is for you. But I'm going to show you a variety of ways that people have come up with, so you and your parent can reflect on which methods will work with your lifestyle.

Making promises to yourself

This is the most common way people set goals. They just think to themselves, *Ya know, one of these days I should get around to washing the car.* This is an extremely popular and extremely ineffective way to set goals.

Why?

There's no accountability. Your thoughts float around and disappear all the time, right? So you set that goal and then next thing you know, you can't actually see out of your car's windshield and you back into a tree. OK, maybe not that extreme.

Telling other people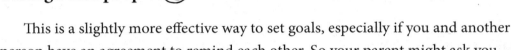

This is a slightly more effective way to set goals, especially if you and another person have an agreement to remind each other. So your parent might ask you, *Can you remind me to go to the carwash after art class?* And you agree. And often, this will work.

The problem with this approach is that it doesn't "scale up." It works for little things that you'd probably remember anyway, but it doesn't work so well for large numbers of things and for more complicated, multi-step goals.

Keeping a public board

Lots of families have a whiteboard or bulletin board in the family area of their house. Your parent might already use one for family "to do" items and planning. If so, you can either stake a claim to part of the board for yourself, or install your own.

The great thing about a public board is that it's right there looking at you all day. It's really easy to put things on it, and equally easy to check them off.

One drawback is that things tend to get moved and changed a lot, so you don't have any record of what you've done. Also, you might forget to look at it, or you might be out of the house a lot and not remember what's on it.

We have a whiteboard that we use a lot. We find that it helps to have daily tasks on the whiteboard, but it doesn't work well for long-term tasks. They tend to get covered up by doodles and erased by accident. So I would recommend having a public board, but would say that you probably want something else for backup.

> I write down my classwork goals every week on a piece of paper and tape it to the wall, but I don't record any of my short term or daily goals. Maybe if I had a daily list it would be easier to stay motivated.
>
> David

Calendars

Whether a print calendar hanging on your wall or a digital calendar that syncs with your devices, calendars can be handy. If you're an "old school" family and don't do digital, then a calendar can help organize things that have to happen on a certain date. So for example, if you need to go to the community college to register for classes, you can look at your calendar, find an empty time, and put it on. Just having something on the calendar makes it more likely you will do it.

I highly recommend moving into the digital age if you can. My family uses shared Google Calendars (which work within our computers' Calendar app as well). We have a calendar for shared family events, a calendar for each child's activities, and even a calendar for reminding us to feed our snake.

All of us have write-access to these calendars. If you're old enough to be using this book, you are old enough to have write privileges on your family calendar. But don't go berserk putting events like "buy a gallon of mint chip ice cream" on it, OK? Shared calendars have to be respected by everyone who is part of them.

The great thing about calendars is that they link tasks to days and times. If you set your digital calendar to ping you when things are supposed to get done, even better. (I started doing this after I not only missed a haircut appointment, but missed the rescheduled appointment, too!)

The drawback to calendars is that once the day has passed, it sort of disappears. So if you don't do something you're supposed to (and not everything gets done when you plan it to, right?), you have to remember to move it forward on the calendar or you can easily forget about it.

A friend of mine suggests that you put a repeating task on your calendar for things that must get done. After five days of being reminded to do the task, you'll be so annoyed, you do it just to get the reminders to stop!

I was having trouble with my piano music so I made a goal to practice longer every day for a week, and it worked! I finally learned the pieces.

Reid

Digital checklist and reminder tools

My last recommendation is to check out the variety of digital tools that now exist for planning and goal-setting. I'll tell you about my system so you get an example, but I'm not saying that you should do it my way.

Calendar reminders

I put small tasks that I pretty much know I'm going to take care of onto our shared calendars with a reminder set. Of course, the reminder comes up on my phone and I can just swipe it away—this is why I only put on tasks that I pretty much am sure I'll get to. If you have a tendency to "swipe and forget," you can set your calendar to repeat the reminder every day. When you've actually done the task, then you can delete the reminder.

Checklist tool

I like to keep tasks that are more important in Wunderlist, a free checklist app. Like a calendar app, it will beep at me—on my computer, my phone, and my tablet!—when something is set to get done.

Unlike a calendar, it doesn't go away when time slides forward (as time has a tendency to do). It keeps at me with a red-circled number on its icon to remind me how many things are overdue. (While I'm writing this, there is a big number 4 in that red circle. Oops!)

Also unlike a calendar, I can keep checklist items that persist but don't remind me of a date. So I have one checklist that's a list of cool videos I've come across that I want to watch with my kids. I don't want to be reminded on a certain date, but I also don't want to forget about them.

Note-taking tool

Finally, I use Evernote, a note-keeping app that syncs between my devices, to keep more verbose plans. We have a shared Evernote folder for each kid's educational planning. The student and both parents can access it and change it. In there we keep notes about future educational ideas, checklists of academic tasks that need to be filled, agreements that we write up, and more.

This is the most flexible tool we use, but it's also the least focused, so that cuts both ways. Evernote has checklist and calendar options, but I like keeping those functions separate. You might want to find one type of software that does it all. It's really up to what works best for you. Chances are, your parent already has some sort of system, so you might start with that. But if you want to devise your own, there are lots of options out there.

My best tool...

The Very Very Best Tool Ever

Did I get your attention?
Ready for a mind-blowing recommendation?

Here it is:

The very, very best tool ever is the one that works best for you. You can take other people's advice to try things out, but in the end, choose what fits in best with your life and keeps you most on track.

Using your tools ✓

You aren't going to decide on a method right now—it will probably slowly evolve as you work on your goal-setting. However, nothing will happen if you don't start, so start today.

Really.

If you already have a tool to use, start using it. If you don't, just randomly choose something, anything, and don't try to find the "perfect" solution. (Why? Because it doesn't exist!)

Once you have your tools in place, you can go about setting and checking off your short-term goals.

Why is it important to check off small achievements?

Good question. It's not necessary, is it? Perhaps you put "take out the garbage" for each Wednesday evening on your calendar, but your parent already reminds you to do it. Maybe you wrote "finish math exam" on your whiteboard right before you went and did it. And you took the time to add "try out art class" on your device's checklist, even though it was already on the calendar.

There are two great reasons to put short-term goals on your checklist:

First, lots of little things tend to slip away when you're busy, and homeschooling can be very busy. So if you write them down, you're just simply more likely to do them.

But more importantly, when you check something off a checklist, it feels great! And then later, you can look back to see what you've accomplished. And much later, when you've forgotten whether you fed a mouse to your snake last weekend, you can look at your checklist and see *yes, I did that.*

The importance of being present

There's something else about keeping tabs on what you're doing: It helps you feel more present in your life. Sometimes it seems like life is just sliding by. It's full of stuff—good stuff, boring stuff, fun stuff, yucky stuff—and you're just riding along on the waves of stuff coming at you.

Sometimes this is fine. But sometimes you feel overwhelmed. You feel like you're not getting anything done. You forget what the point is.

Keeping tabs on what your small goals are can actually help you feel better. When doing household chores is keeping you from your favorite game, it would be nice to feel a little better about it. When you've got fifteen things to do before you can get out of the house to go hang out with your friends, checking them off shows your progress and makes you feel like you're not just "doing time."

📲 Exercise 2a: Check it off!

Think of a small thing you've been meaning to do that takes no preparation and requires no help from others or materials you don't have. Set it as a goal by putting it on your calendar or checklist. Meet the goal within two days. You should write the deadline on your calendar even if you're sure you won't forget. Make sure to mark your checklist when you're done!

📲 Exercise 2b: Something you already know how to do

Think of a skill that you learned in the last month. It can be academic (math, writing, etc.) or in any other domain (sports, art, etc.). Write down a goal of performing that skill, then document yourself doing it within one week. Check it off!

Stretchercize 2: Sharing with others

Choose one of these exercises which involve other people.

1) Go do a household chore that you really don't like to do. Do it quickly, well, and without complaining, then tell your parent what you did. You might want to be holding a camera to catch the shocked look on your parent's face!

2) Using art supplies that you have on hand, create a picture of your pet or a type of animal you like. Your goal here is to complete the picture, not worry if it looks good to you! Share it with someone in person or via email.

3) Set up a video camera and record yourself doing a skill from a sport you enjoy. Upload the video and email the link to friends or family.

 Recap: In this chapter, we • • •

- • • defined one-step goals
- • • discussed why we set short-term goals
- • • looked at examples of ways to set short-term goals
- • • discussed using tools to keep track of our goals
- • • discussed why is it important to notice when you've achieved small goals
- • • discussed the importance of being present

Onward!

CHAPTER 3
Two-step goals

You may delay, but time will not.

—**Benjamin Franklin**

Examples of two-step goals

Two-step goals are goals that are pretty immediate, but there's something stopping us from doing it Right Now. Maybe we don't have the materials on hand. Maybe it requires someone else's involvement. In any case, these goals are just a little harder to achieve than the ones we did in the last chapter.

Here are some two-step goals I've achieved recently:

1. I figured out how to register my son for his first community college class. In this case, I was relying on the college's website, which seemed incomplete, so I had to wait until their office was open to call for the information I needed in order to proceed.

2. I made dinner yesterday. We didn't have the ingredients I needed so I added them to my device's checklist. When I was out taking my child to an appointment, I went to the store and bought the ingredients.

3. I posted some information I'd forgotten to say in class on my class's online forum. This was a two-step process because I only remembered that I'd forgotten at bedtime. (This often happens to me!) So I scribbled

a reminder to myself and left it by the bathroom sink (where I go every morning). That was the first step. The second step happened the next morning when I was brushing my teeth. I saw the note, carried it to my computer, and posted the message on the forum.

Notice that I have three different types of two-step goals here:

#1 was a checklist item. I got to click that little checkbox on my checklist. Yay!

#2 was one of those small, two-step goals that face us all day long. I just kept it in my head, though I did add the items to my shopping list.

#3 was a goal that involved reporting back to other people. I didn't put it on a checklist, but I knew that the other people were depending on me to pass on the information.

Two-step goals are easier to put off

I bet you already know why this is. Yep, there's something standing in the way between you and the goal:

- You don't have information that you need
- You don't have materials that you need
- It requires someone else's involvement
- You have to go somewhere to do it

The thing is, two-step goals aren't necessarily any more difficult than one-step goals—they're just much easier to procrastinate on.

That's why I always recommend that when you recognize that you've got a two-step goal in front of you, your first instinct should be to add it to your calendar or a checklist.

We call them "instincts," but humans, unlike other animals, don't just operate on instinct. Our lives are way too complex. We "create" something like instinct by instilling habits. And the way to instill habits, research has found, is to force yourself to do the thing at least 3 times in a row.

If you keep letting 2-step goals slide, you'll never develop the instinct/habit to get them done.

What are habits? In your brain, particular things are happening that form habits. Our brains work by making connections between existing memories, skills, and knowledge. This is the reason why humans are capable of doing so much. If you have a tile floor in a cold climate, you probably developed the habit of putting on slippers just by freezing your feet a few times. In your brain, that habit consists of connections that were formed by repetition. It's actually pretty easy to form a habit--just do it a few times until it feels natural. Breaking a bad habit that you already formed, however, can be much more difficult!

Goals as building-blocks

You probably already noticed this: even the smallest goals are made up of smaller goals. It's like Zeno's Paradox: You can keep breaking down goals into smaller and smaller pieces until you get to ridiculously tiny actions that you don't even have to think about. (First, breathe in, then, breathe out!)

Each goal is often built of other smaller goals, and each goal is often part of a larger goal. Let's look at my examples:

1. Figuring out how to register my son for a community college class is obviously not an "end" goal in itself. Clearly, the long-term goal here is for my

son to be successful in community college and pursue some of his home-school education that way.

2. Making dinner is a relatively complex task that is mostly made up of things I no longer even notice as I do them. Most kids, when they are making a recipe, need the recipe to tell them to preheat the oven if needed. When I'm cooking, instinct/habit tells me to turn on the oven when I need to. So the "goal" of making dinner, which is part of the larger goal of maintaining a happy, healthy family, is made up of all sorts of little goals I don't even have to think about. The one task that took thought, and thus needed to go on my checklist, was going to the store.

3. Posting a piece of information for my class was also not an end-goal. It was part of the larger goal of presenting my students with a class that served their needs and guided them in learning the topic at hand.

Each of my goals in these examples were built of smaller goals, and also are building blocks themselves of larger goals.

The goal of goal-setting, then, is to create habits which make many of our actions in meeting goals simply instinctive—if we had to think about each and every building block, we'd go nuts!

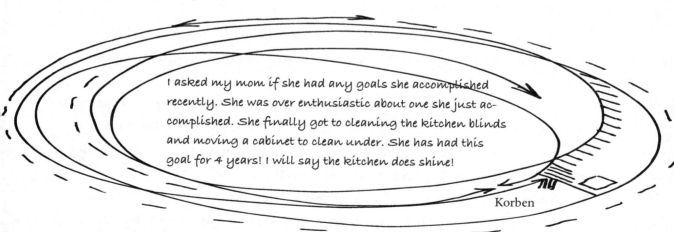

I asked my mom if she had any goals she accomplished recently. She was over enthusiastic about one she just accomplished. She finally got to cleaning the kitchen blinds and moving a cabinet to clean under. She has had this goal for 4 years! I will say the kitchen does shine!

Korben

Homeschooling and the ease of procrastination

I started this book by reminding you that you are not a sheep. You probably knew that. And even the most rule-following, crowd-adapted person on this planet is still not a sheep. We all do exercise free will on occasion.

Homeschooling is simply different than schooling, however. In school, much of what you do is done because it is presented to you as a fait accompli (that's "done deal" in French). You have very little choice about what you do day-to-day if you're going to school.

Homeschooling offers a lot of choice, and therein lies the danger. The more choice you have, the easier it is to procrastinate. And procrastination is the number one reason why people don't meet their goals.

In the last chapter I asked you to think of something you'd been "meaning to do." Do you have a lot of those "mean to do"s piled up? If you do, it's likely that you have a tendency toward procrastination.

If you have a tendency toward procrastination, and you're a homeschooler, and you have things you really want to do in your life, you've got a perfect recipe for disaster. But if you add goal-setting to that recipe, it suddenly shifts to a recipe for success.

We're going to address "success" in depth in Chapter 5, so just hold that thought for now. Just know that "success" doesn't mean that I'm promising you fame and wealth!

What I am promising you is that procrastination is a habit, and habits can be changed. In the last twenty years, lots of research has been done on the human brain. And since people have always wondered why some people are more motivated than others, they've been studying motivation.

What's clear is that we are all able to develop new habits—teens are even better than anyone else at it because your brain is already is a major state of change. So procrastination is just another habit. Decide it's one you're doing away with, act on that decision, and you'll see change.

By the way, not all procrastination is created equal. Lots of activities involve healthy procrastination. Two scientists got a Nobel Prize for what happened when they were amusing themselves by playing with cellophane tape and pencil lead.

In other words, no one is telling you to be a drudge. Notice which types of procrastination are leading you away from your goals, and that's what you should address first.

I always feel like my mom is nagging me to do my homework when I am much better at getting it done at the last minute. I have a procrastination monkey in my head that steers me away from the things that are really important, such as math and homework. I really want to get rid of it, but I don't know how! Maybe frighten it with daily deadlines?   Megan

Homeschooling organizational methods that help with goal-setting

In Chapter 2 I detailed my own personal method for organization. That was meant neither as an endorsement of the commercial products I named, nor a recommendation that you adopt a system that at all resembles mine.

You need to organize your life in a way that makes sense for you and for your life. For example, I have heard of really messy people hiring professional organizers to clean out their homes. However, I suspect that a professional organizer could actually make the situation worse by not taking care to devise a system that works for that messy person.

Rather than comparing yourself to someone you know who's the most organized, neatest, most together person around, simply look at yourself and decide what would work for you.

The Messy Student

Is your room a complete disaster? Do you often lose things you need? Things you actually don't want to lose?

If yes, then you need to start small. Choose a place where you always put your academic work, and put a repeating event on your calendar to clean and reorganize that spot every single week.

Every week? Are you kidding?

Nope.

Organized people make a habit of organizing on a regular basis. You need to force yourself to learn the habit at least to organize one place that really matters to your education.

The Forgetful Student

Do you forget to go into your online class because you're playing games? Do you arrive at a class without the homework you spent hours on? Do you depend on your parent to remind you about many things?

You need to develop new habits that will help you take charge of your own education. How can you argue that you deserve to have more say in what you're doing for your homeschooling if you need your parent to be there reminding you of things all the time?

I have a confession to make: I'm a bit forgetful. On a regular basis, I leave the house, back out of the driveway, drive down the road a ways, then go back once I remember what I've forgotten. And this is true even though I am pretty good at using various methods I've set up. When I forget, though, it's because I fall back on the old habit of "oh, I don't need to check my list," rather than following my rules.

First of all, create a place near the door that you use to exit the house. This is where you will put things that you need to take with you. If you attend community college or go to classes outside of the house, this will be invaluable to you. Remember to put things there as you remember them, so that you don't have to remember everything at the last minute.

Second, modern digital tools are going to be very useful for you. If you have a device that you carry with you, make sure to set it up so that it gives you reminders that you will listen to. Make sure to use software that syncs between devices if you use a different device at home.

If you don't use digital tools, then a good old paper planner works great. Sticky notes are also a fabulous invention—but you do have to remember to put them up, and remember to look at them. No matter what you use, make sure to *use* it—most forgetful people are only forgetful because they forget to consult all the lists they've made to remind themselves!

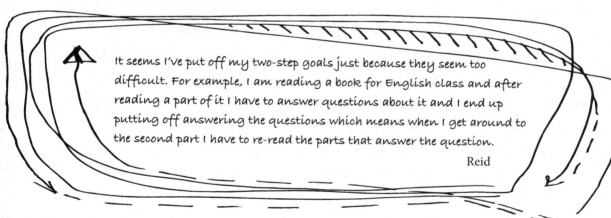

It seems I've put off my two-step goals just because they seem too difficult. For example, I am reading a book for English class and after reading a part of it I have to answer questions about it and I end up putting off answering the questions which means when I get around to the second part I have to re-read the parts that answer the question.

Reid

The Overly Busy Student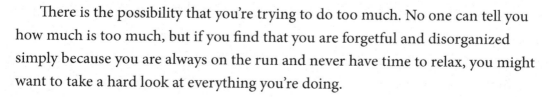

There is the possibility that you're trying to do too much. No one can tell you how much is too much, but if you find that you are forgetful and disorganized simply because you are always on the run and never have time to relax, you might want to take a hard look at everything you're doing.

Yes, it's true, the modern teen feels pressured to do everything and, what's more, to be good at everything. Very few people are really able to achieve this level of performance, however, and it's no shame to admit that you have gone too far. Considering your long-term goals helps you focus on what matters to you and to your goals, and you can learn to disregard a lot of the noise.

A little more about habit

I keep mentioning habit, which is different from instinct. Instinct is when you duck your head to avoid getting hit by a ball flying at your face. Habit is catching that ball and throwing it to the second base to get the other team out. Instinct is part of how our brain works naturally; habit is how it works once we've trained it.

Habits are formed over time. They are easier to form than to break, as any smoker or overeater will tell you. But you can form new, healthy habits and break old, unhealthy ones.

I decided that it was important to me to stop using disposable bags at the grocery store. But I kept forgetting to bring my reusable bags in. One day, totally frustrated at myself for forgetting again, I made a resolution: Each time I forgot my bags, I would embarrass myself: I'd go up to a checker, let them know that my cart wasn't abandoned, and go get the darn bags.

Magically, after three times of this, I stopped forgetting my bags. Now it feels weird to go into a grocery store without bags in my hands.

That's habit. (Not magic.)

Set up your goal-setting system

Last year I attended a local writer's conference for the first time. It turned out that they had a tradition: At the end of the conference, everyone would write one goal on two pieces of paper. Then we lined up, walked past the roaring fireplace, and threw in one of the pieces of paper. We were instructed to post the other piece of paper where we could see it when we work.

It was a pretty dramatic ceremony, a bit more drama than I usually am drawn to. But believe it or not, this year I attended the conference again and I could happily report that I had fulfilled my goal! It turned out that the drama, which I wasn't too excited about, did give me a little kick.

Group Systems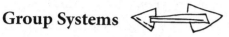

If you are doing goal-setting with a group, you may decide to do something formal and dramatic like this. (Drama tends to work better when you have an audience!) You might decide that everyone should report back on a schedule, share ideas and encouragement on an online bulletin board, or complete tasks as a group.

You might also decide that your group wants to be less formal, so that you just get together and chat about what you are doing to improve your goal-setting.

In any case, one of the nice things about doing things as a group is the accountability: your group should make sure that you have some way of sharing what your goals are, which steps you have taken toward them, and when you complete or abandon them.

Personal Systems

I predict that most of us are going it alone or just with a parent or sibling. In that case, make sure that you remember that groups make accountability easier. You're going to have to work a little harder to stay on task without a group cheering you on.

If you are devising a personal system, make sure that it has accountability. For example, this could be your personal system:

1. Write a goal on your whiteboard with a planned date of completion
2. Write the steps below the goal and check them off as you do them
3. Erase the goal only when it's completed or abandoned

Positives of this approach? You've chosen a public place to state your goal, so your family can help you along. You have broken your goal into smaller steps. You have a physical action—checking things off—that will help you feel good about taking the small steps.

Challenges with this approach? Well, when you choose a public place to keep track of your goal, make sure everyone else knows not to erase it! Also, this system doesn't do anything to remind you on a daily basis, so remember to look at the whiteboard. (That may sound funny, but we often "stop seeing" things that are familiar.)

Overall, it's not a bad plan. But you might want to refine it:

1. You could add calendar reminders on your device so that each day you get a reminder.
2. You could officially ask your family to ask after your progress, or notice when you've checked something off so they can celebrate your progress.
3. You could post your goal also in a private place so that you think about it when you're not in the kitchen.

A note about family conflict 😦 😊

Why discuss family conflict in a book about goal-setting? Well, you're home-schoolers, so you're with your family more than other kids. And it's likely that at least one parent feels largely responsible for your education, and perhaps another parent isn't so involved but sometimes has input as well.

Becoming self-sufficient is your major pursuit at your age, and it might feel like parents and siblings are in your way. Why are they always criticizing what you're doing? Why are they always bugging you about the goal you've written on the whiteboard when it's not even near the completion date? Why is your sibling laughing at you or making you feel like you aren't as accomplished? Why does your parent seem to hold you to higher standards than your sibling is held to?

None of these frustrations are new. Families—even the most functional, loving,

48

happiest families—have to deal with conflict.

The first thing to remember is that conflict is normal and healthy. Don't feel bad about it unless it's making you feel bad.

If the conflict is making you feel bad, the worst thing you can do is not talk about it. Maybe talking about it feels scary, but talking about it is the only way it's going to end.

When you do talk about it, try to remember that it's your problem, so you have to own it. Start your sentences with "I feel" and not "You are doing this to me."

If you feel like your family conflict is more than you can handle, seek help from an adult you trust. That can be a teacher you work with, an extended family member, a counselor, a friend of your parent, or someone in your religious organization. Again, remember to use "I" statements because your job isn't to "fix" your family—your job is to find a way to live the healthiest, most successful life possible within the craziness than life throws at all of us.

⏵ Exercise 3a: Cut'n'Paste

Make a list of the things you like to do. Cut them into individual slips of paper and arrange them in 5 or fewer piles by theme (for example, "sports," "arts," "group activities" "solo activities"). Using a big sheet of paper, write the themes in different spots on the paper and put big circles around each one so there's room inside the circle for more writing. Using different colored pens, go to each circle and write in all the activities you enjoy in that theme. In a different-colored ink, write in activities you would like to learn to do within each theme, if there are any.

⏵ Exercise 3b: Get out of the house

Think of something you want to do that involves one trip to a store or the library—somewhere out of the house. Write down the activity as a goal with the steps you need to take to achieve it. (There may be more than two steps, but it should be something that really only takes two big steps.) Achieve the goal and check it off in one week.

 ## Stretchercize 3: Small goal interview

Choose someone to interview (an adult or teen is probably best). Ask them about something small—a short-term goal—they have achieved recently, and how they did it. To make sure they understand, give them these examples: "I finally got around to cleaning out my closet," "I took a small but necessary step for my career that I had been avoiding," "I helped a friend." Write up the steps they took.

 ## Recap: In this chapter, we . . .

- • • looked at examples of two-step goals
- • • discussed why these goals are easier to put off than one-step goals
- • • looked at goals as building-blocks
- • • talked about how easy it is for homeschoolers to procrastinate
- • • looked at organizational methods that help with goal-setting
- • • set up a preliminary goal-setting system
- • • discussed family conflict

Onward!

CHAPTER 4
Multi-Step Goals

 Over every mountain there is a path, although it may not be seen from the valley.

—Theodore Roethke

Climbing a sheer rock face

Have you ever gone rock-climbing or climbed on a climbing wall at a park? Then you know that feeling of standing in front of a vertical wall, looking up and thinking, *Really? I'm going to climb up there?*

What happens next? Some kids will just back away and find something else to do. That's legitimate in this case—kids who don't have the strength to take on that big of a challenge might be better off finding an easier activity and working up to it.

But what usually happens next is obvious. You look up at the top, which looks insurmountable. Then you look down near your foot and there it is, the first place you can step. Then you look slightly up from your head and there it is, the first hand grip you can reach. You step, you grip, and you're up.

One down, many to go.

Multi-step goals = a series of smaller goals

Remember this: no matter what you plan to do, you always have to take the first step in order to get to the end.

You will never get there if you just stand still gazing at the end goal, so far away.

Goals will remain unattainable if you see them as one impossibly long stretch up to the top.

Any goal can be chopped up into smaller, more easily attainable goals. And there is always more than one path to get to a goal that's further away.

Let's look at a fictional student's goal: to study computer science at a good university. This student is fourteen and in ninth grade. Those good universities seem to be at the top of a sheer wall of rock.

But this is actually a goal that has some relatively clear paths.

One path would be to go to the well-regarded technical magnet school nearby. But our homeschooler immediately decides against that. She's a self-starter and prefers doing things her own way.

Another path is to study everything at home and hope that she can prove herself to universities when she applies. But she looks at the admission requirements of some of the universities she's interested in and sees that they actually have some specific requirements in the areas of math and science. She decides self-study alone isn't the path she wants to take.

She finds out that she can take the math she needs at her local community college. She's not sure she's going to be able to handle the workload, though, and the first math class she needs is supposedly the hardest class offered at the college. Scary sheer rock face? Not at all. She finds another class in a subject she enjoys, biology, that seems like a less daunting challenge. She decides if she does well in bio, she'll take another step up and try math. She likes the face-to-face interaction of college and its accountability factor.

Having decided on this path, she realizes that it is made up of a variety of potential paths. An online math school she's taken a class from in the past just got certified to offer the courses she needs, as well. So if the college doesn't work out, she has a different option. Also, the college has an honors transfer program—if she doesn't get into a university she likes as a freshman, she can try again as a transfer.

Set goals that actually are attainable

One thing that people often forget to do is look at their goals and question whether they are actually attainable.

What? Are you saying that I can't do anything I put my mind to?

No, actually I'm not. But I am saying that sometimes people think they've set a goal for themselves, but it actually depends on other people's cooperation in order to succeed. And other people have this way of not behaving themselves!

Let's take another look at our budding computer scientist above. Let's say that she has a similar goal, but it's more focused. Sounds good, right? But here's her goal:

"I want to study Computer Science at Stanford University with the eminent Professor Demetrius Smith."

(Yes, I did make up Dr. Smith. My apologies if such a Dr. Smith actually exists!)

What's wrong with her more focused goal? Isn't it better to have focused goals?

Yes and no. It's great that she knows what she wants, but suddenly she's cut off lots of options. Stanford University has one of the lowest acceptance rates of all universities. Every year they turn away thousands of highly qualified students. By limiting herself to Stanford alone, she has put the attainment of her goal directly into the hands of the Admissions Committee at Stanford, people who don't know her and don't understand that their job is to help her attain her goal. (Darn them!)

Furthermore, the year she applies that sneaky Dr. Smith decides that he hates sunshine and silicon and has taken a position at a rural university in Norway. Darn that Dr. Smith for paying attention to his own personal goals!

Notice that the initial goal we set up was dependent on her hard work, focus, research into good CS programs, and performance on tests. These are all things she has some measure of control over.

If you always set goals that are unattainable, you will always feel like you are failing. That is not a good way to live your life.
Josie

Here's another example: There was a young man who loved rock and roll, and he wanted to be a rock star. Notice: He didn't just want to play rock and roll. His "goal" was to be the cream of the crop. Of course, he had very little control over this "goal" (that's why I put it in quotes—it was actually just a dream!), and focusing on it had some negative effects. First, he didn't enjoy playing music anymore, because he was never getting the adulation he thought he should be getting. Second, he didn't put in the work he needed to in order to succeed because his goal wasn't simply to make a living as a musician (attainable), but rather to choose for the public and music executives who they think should be the next star (unattainable).

Why do we dream about unattainable things? I want you to think right now about something you dream about that's probably never going to happen. Don't worry, I'm not going to ask you to write it down or tell someone. We all have dreams, and sometimes these dreams are preposterous! Is this a bad thing? Not at all. Our dreams allow us to explore ideas in a world without limits. It's really great that our guitar player dreams about being a rock star—it helps him work hard on his guitar technique. Dreams often lead to real-world successes, as long as we don't fixate on the dream to the exclusion of things we really can accomplish.

When you set a goal, make sure that it really is a goal that you can achieve. Yes, shoot for your dreams, but don't waste your time waiting for unattainable goals to happen to you when you can make attainable goals a reality every day.

Keep focused on the building blocks

I hope you don't feel like I'm shooting down your dreams. At your age, you should dream. But reality tends to get in the way of dreams if you don't work on them every day.

And the way you work on them is by focusing on your building blocks. You know what's going to happen if all you do is dream that you got an A in algebra, but you don't do any work. That A is probably not going to happen. The building blocks for an A in algebra are pretty clear: do the homework conscientiously, talk to your teacher, tutor, or parent if you start to get lost, use other resources to make sure you understand the concepts, prepare well for tests, and don't choke when the test comes around.

Maybe one of those building blocks is really hard for you. You're taking a class with a local teacher and you find the teacher sort of, well, incomprehensible. You talk to him and he sounds like he's speaking a foreign language. What do you do?

Always remember that for each building block that you can't use, there's probably another you can try. Maybe you can get help from a friend who's already aced the class. Maybe you can go online and get explanations that make sense for you. Maybe you need to drop the class and try with another teacher.

It's really important to see the building blocks as raw material for reaching your goal, not as walls you have to climb over. If your goal is to learn to speak French fluently by the time you fly to Paris in June, then, sorry to say, you are going to have to memorize the necessary vocabulary. But there are different ways to get words to stick in your head, and if one doesn't work for you, try another.

The building blocks are there to keep you focused on attainable goals rather than unattainable ones. "Get fluent in French in six months" seems really daunting. But "learn all the vocabulary words in Chapter Six by Friday" is a lot more doable. And becoming fluent in French is built up in increments like this.

Goal-setting accountability ⩔ ⩔ ⩔

One of the big problems with focusing on the building blocks is that sometimes we don't notice that we're not actually working on them. We feel busy, but when we look back at our week or month, we find that there's been no progress.

This is where accountability comes in. In Chapter 3 we talked about various systems to help you keep track of your goals. Did you set up a system?

If not, go back and read it again!

You need to be held accountable in one way or another or you're probably not going to get this goal-setting thing.

Make sure that your accountability system is something that happens on a daily or weekly basis. Most of us can't focus on something that takes up to a month without any way to note progress.

Our computer science student has a master list of steps she needs to take, and every time she's feeling down or unsure of herself, she can go to that list and find an item to check off.

Make a list of 20 universities that offer programs I might like. CHECK!

Put a reminder on my calendar to sign up for the SAT next year. CHECK!

Notice that our budding rock and roll star can't really create that checklist. "Be a rock star" doesn't really lend itself to items you can check off a list. But if he adjusted his goal to "get together a band of musicians at my skill level and get some gigs," at least he could have a set of building blocks that he can work on.

Celebrating achievements of the building blocks

Remember a major reason to keep checklists: It feels so darn great to click that little checkbox!

And when you include other people in your goals, you can get great positive feedback for your little building block successes. That's why so many people who are trying to lose weight, exercise, build new businesses, and learn complex skills seek out groups to join.

The human brain loves that feeling of pay-off. Did you know that there's actually a physical reaction in your brain when you get that YES! feeling? That's your brain releasing chemicals that make it feel great, which is our brain's way of saying, "Keep doing that! You're cool!"

So don't be afraid to celebrate your little achievements.

It's not bragging. Bragging is what braggarts do to feel like they're better than other people. Celebrating small achievements is a way of sharing our pleasure with other people. If nothing else, make sure to tell your parent when you feel like you just finished something hard, something you had resisted, or something that ended up being fun after all.

And parents, if you're reading this, please take these opportunities to offer encouragement to your kids. Your teens might just grunt and shrug, but your support does mean a lot to them. (Right?)

I can't set goals very well because I don't trust myself in deciding whether I can attain them.
Reid

Hone your homeschool organizational method

At this point you might be noticing some problems. Maybe you decided to keep a physical checklist, but you lost it. Maybe you decided to use some fancy new software you got, but you just can't figure it out.

Maybe you lost this book and you've just found it again after three months when your parent told you it was time to clean out your room or you'd have to go live in the doghouse!

There is nothing wrong with admitting that something isn't working. In fact, learning to adjust your routine is an important part of becoming responsible for yourself. A lot of us have trouble with this. Some of us are on the autism spectrum and we become uncomfortable when we try to change routines. Some of us don't want to face things that feel challenging and uncomfortable.

But you can celebrate your building-block "failures" just like you celebrate your successes. Think of it this way: You know something isn't working, and that's a great thing to know! Now go fix it.

Reread the suggestions in Chapter 3 and see if there's a different way you might approach your organizational methods. If not, ask people you know who are organized to share their ideas, watch videos, read books… There are many ideas out there and at least one of them will work for you.

Critique your goal-setting system

At this point, if you've been doing the exercises, you've set a few goals and hopefully attained them. You've written them on your whiteboard or put them on your checklist. You've broken them down into steps.

I hope you've also been inspired to look at your "real life" (outside of the exercises in this book) in a new way.

In any case, you now have a few experiences to work with. The first exercise below will ask you to take a closer look at what you've done. Once you've done that, feel very free to adjust the way you are doing things.

Maybe you need to split very small goals into even smaller ones. Go for it!

Maybe you really get annoyed at having to check off too many items, so you need to chunk your goals into bigger pieces. OK!

At your age, you are in the process of "maturing." And maturity is, in part, understanding yourself and how you work.

58

Sometimes maturity means making a change in yourself.

Sometimes maturity means understanding, accepting, and working around an attribute that you don't feel you can change right now.

But maturity always involves taking responsibility for your life and your actions. As we discussed earlier, that's what homeschooling as a teen is all about. So now is the time to reflect on whether you are working toward that goal.

Exercise 4a: Reflection

Look at the goals you have set since you started this book. Answer these questions:

Which goal was the most fun?

Which goal was the easiest?

Which goal was the hardest?

Did you fail to meet a goal? Why?

Were any of your goals part of reaching a more long-term goal?

If yes, do you feel like you are closer to meeting that long-term goal?

Have you reevaluated any goals and changed or abandoned them?

Do you feel like these exercises have been helpful to you? Why or why not?

Exercise 4b: This year's goal

Choose a goal that you need to meet this year. Some examples might be passing Algebra, advancing to a new level in your sport, or finishing a short film. Write down the steps that you need to go through in order to get there. Remember that something like "passing Algebra" seems like a one-step goal, but it involves steps that you take each day and week: doing homework, arriving on time to class (if you're taking one), getting help if you start getting lost, identifying lagging skills so you can improve them, passing the final exam. Identify the major steps and create accountability for each one, such as reporting hours of homework completed each week or keeping a checklist of steps to take.

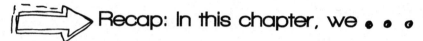 Stretchercize 4: Career steps

Interview an adult who has a career that interests you. Find out the steps they took to get to their career. Be sure to ask them whether they feel like they always went in a straight line toward their goal or whether they wandered around a bit. (You might be surprised at the answer!)

Recap: In this chapter, we • • •

- • • discussed why these goals can look more daunting
- • • focused on small goals as building blocks
- • • discussed goal-setting accountability
- • • discussed the importance of celebrating achievements of the building blocks
- • • honed your homeschool organizational method
- • • critiqued your goal-setting system

Onward!

CHAPTER 5

Homeschool Success

Success is not the key to happiness. Happiness is the key to success.
If you love what you are doing, you will be successful.

—**Albert Schweitzer**

What is "success"?

If you're growing up in the United States, you are accustomed to thinking of success as a combination of fame and money. Our mass media sells this and other rather destructive ideas. Why? Because these ideas sell, and they're self-reinforcing. People in our media want to be successful at what they do, and one measure of success is making the most money possible.

You can probably come up with other damaging ideas of success. Girls have probably noticed that they get a lot of pressure to look attractive (according to a narrow definition of "attractive"). People of color have probably noticed pressure to act or look "white" in order to succeed. Those of you growing up in rural areas might have heard the line that you have to go somewhere "important" to succeed.

All of these ideas of success are damaging because they ask us to deny something about the core of who we are and what we want. Success has nothing to do with denying who we are. In fact, most successful people would say that they are successful in part because they were able to stay true to themselves.

So what is success if not money and fame? Well, sometimes success does come with money and fame, but only in pursuits that happen to have money or fame as part of their core.

Success is defined by you: who you are, what you want, and why you want it. If you are an artist, chances are you feel great practicing your art. It makes you feel fulfilled. You may also feel that you are making statements to the world about things you believe. So in that case, money (although always appreciated by artists) does not equal success.

What if, in order to get money, all you have to do is draw ugly drawings of dogs with drooling tongues? For some reason, people will pay you tons of money for those drawings, yet you feel like a piece of your soul is sucked out each time you make one.

That's not success. ⇐ = = =

For our budding computer scientist in the last chapter, success looks like going to one of the top computer science departments. But two things happen along the way: First, she doesn't get top grades in her math classes. She does fine, but not well enough to get into Stanford. (Thank goodness she didn't tie herself to that narrow goal. Also, she really doesn't want to live in Norway!)

But she *loved* her biology class! She felt like the world opened up its secrets to her. And something she really loved about it was doing computer modeling of biological systems. She realized she needed to take a new look at her list of universities. She found one with a program that allowed her to design her own major. It turned out to be a great place for her and she flourished.

Success! ⇐ = = =

Our rock-n-roller from the last chapter had a friend, by the way, who also dreamed of being a rock star. But instead of fixating on the dream (rock star), he set a goal to make his living through music. He started a band, and they did pretty well. Along the way, however, he realized he didn't like traveling so much, but he really liked the technical side of recording music.

While he was a working musician, he'd made contacts in the recording industry. He retooled his goal, took some community college classes, and became a recording engineer, a satisfying career for him.

Success!

Working toward our goals (while feeling free to dream along the way), leads us to success.

Attributes that pave the road to success

There is no single path to any goal, and even less so toward something as hard to define as "success." But there are certain attributes you can cultivate in yourself that will make success more attainable.

⟶ Flexibility

I've mentioned a few times that flexibility is a key skill in goal-setting. The fact is, we change our goals all the time. Sometimes we change because we have to (pool closed due to thunderstorm). Sometimes we change because we want to (wow, biology is cool!).

I read once that researchers found that children growing up in cities who don't ever get a chance to walk in the country don't learn the skill of walking on rough ground. When you put these kids in a lumpy field, they fall down. They have to learn a weird skill that comes naturally to us country folks, where your ankles, knees, and hips are ready to flex in one direction or another as you walk.

Life for many little kids is more like a nicely paved sidewalk, because adults around them are dealing with the lumps and bumps. When you were little, you may not have even noticed when your parent had to go without some favorite magazines and foods because money was tight. You may not have noticed that the real reason that you moved to a new town was that your parent lost a job.

But now that you're embarking on your own across that field, you're going to start noticing the lumps. Flexibility is key to dealing with them. Have goals, yes, but don't get so fixated on them that you fall down at the first lump you meet.

> I am somewhat flexible. I am severely lacking in grit and focus. I don't minimize bad stress and maximize good stress. I don't think I have a positive use of failure. I also don't think I am very happy over-all.
> Josh

Grit

Grit has received a lot of attention lately because some researchers noticed that people who give up quickly don't reach their goals as often. That seems pretty obvious, doesn't it? But it doesn't necessarily feel obvious in life. Obstacles and disappointments arise, and we can't necessarily see past them and know that we're going to do OK.

People who have grit don't just give up when they hit obstacles. Think about "gritting your teeth": that's something you do when you're about to face a big physical challenge, right?

Personal "grit" is what people have when they are willing to face challenges and overcome them.

> I don't like doing very hard tasks, and I usually give up when I don't get it the first time (unless I really want to complete the thing, or if there's something fun after it). I think having more grit would help me with doing tough tasks.
> Megan

Grit and flexibility sort of look like they're opposites, don't they? Isn't flexibility sort of about giving up—going around or changing directions when an obstacle arises?

I like to think of grit and flexibility as two friends who have two very different strengths. Those two friends can get much more done together because they cooperate and help each other. Grit and flexibility are both important, and have to be used as needed.

→ Focus

Focus is the ability not to get distracted. Again, it's sort of in opposition to grit and flexibility, but it makes a good trio with them. People who focus on their goals tend to be more successful because they don't get distracted. But people who *hyper*-focus—think so obsessively and narrowly that they can't see what else is happening around them—tend not to be as successful.

Hyper-focus is an attribute often seen in people on the autism spectrum or with ADHD. If you have been diagnosed with one of these, though, remember that it's just another challenge that you have to face. Nothing is an impassable barrier if you choose to find a way around it.

It really depends on how interested I am in my goal. I can be incredibly focused to the point where I don't really notice the world around me and I can be easily distracted and end up focusing on something completely irrelevant to my goal. If something really bores me, I have to pause every five or ten minutes to do something interesting, like read a few pages of a book or draw something. I think if I set myself the goal of doing something I don't really like for a solid chunk of time without getting up to do something more interesting, I might learn to be more focused.   Laye

→ Humor

I will finish my list of attributes with one that I think is really very important: we have to be able to laugh about ourselves and our lives if we're going to be comfortable and happy (in other words, successful). Life throws a lot of ridiculous things in front of us, and it really helps to be able to laugh at them, whether alone or in the company of family and friends.

If you have trouble finding humor in life, you might want to ask yourself why, and whether you want to change that. I'll never forget an interview with the writer Maya Angelou in which she said that the thing she most appreciated about Martin Luther King, Jr. was his sense of humor. Amidst all the great things he did for the world, she chose to speak about how he loved to tell jokes.

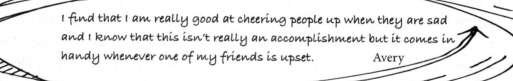

I find that I am really good at cheering people up when they are sad and I know that this isn't really an accomplishment but it comes in handy whenever one of my friends is upset.   Avery

Stress 😞

One of the things that striving for success seems to do for teens these days is to introduce stress into their lives. In fact, teens now report being more stressed than teens have ever felt, as far as we know.

This isn't good, right?

You bet it's not good, and it's led to kids mistreating their bodies and mistreating each other.

One of the great things about homeschooling, however, is that you can monitor your stress level and modify activities that introduce too much stress. Teens in very competitive high schools report getting only a few hours' sleep each night. You can make sure that you get enough sleep by choosing which activities to spend time on. Teens in school might feel pressure to do things that don't align with their goals. As a homeschooler, you can resist that.

It's important to recognize when bad stress is taking a toll on you. You can get some great guidelines for how to identify and deal with stress on KidsHealth.com/teen/ (type "stress" into their search box). Homeschoolers get stressed out just like school kids, and if you are feeling it you need to identify it and get help. Reaching for your goals does not mean you have to suffer extreme mental and physical stress.

Part of the reasons that I quit school was because I stressed out a lot. Now I don't stress as much so this is under control.   Lucas

"Good" Stress 😊

Not enough people seem to talk about good stress. Wait, how can stress be *good*? It turns out that the thing we call stress is just the bad side of something our bodies developed for good purposes.

Imagine you are living in a prehistoric hunter/gatherer society and you exit the forest to see a lion. The lion meets your eyes and crouches. What happens?

Your heart rate goes up to pump oxygen to your muscles.

Your brain activates the "fight or flight center," which decides whether you should stick it out or run.

You don't have a weapon, so you choose to run.

Your body releases chemicals that spur you into action!

You run into the forest, swing up into a tree, and hide out with the monkeys until the lion has gone.

That's some pretty darn *good* stress! Without the adrenaline, the pumping heart, and the quick action of your brain, you'd be lion food.

These days most of us aren't running from lions. But our bodies still respond to stress in the same physical way. Today, the equivalent of running-from-a-lion stress is the excited feeling you get when you're giving a musical performance, or the confident energy you feel when you know you're well-prepared to take a test.

The trick is to learn to recognize when stress has gone to the dark side and deal with it.

How can you tell the difference? If the physical effects of good and bad stress are the same, doesn't that make it hard to figure out which it is? Actually, no. Instead of focusing on the stress itself, focus on the outcome. When you felt stressed out, did you retreat from what you were trying to do and feel like a failure? Bad stress. Did the stress motivate you to do your best? Good stress. Did your performance suffer because of the stress? Bad stress. Did you come out of a hard situation feeling energized? Good stress.

The importance of failure ☹

When you were learning to walk, you were such a failure! First you tried to pull yourself up on a chair but you fell down. Then you tried to pull yourself up by your dog's tail and the dog ran away. Finally you figured out how to stand, but then every time you took a step, you fell down.

Geez, what a failure you were!

Oh, wait, you learned to walk? Everyone who doesn't have a physical disability learns to walk, and the way we learn is from failure. We test out the world to find out which structures will support our weight. We learn to balance our bodies and align our feet.

But at some point in your childhood, you may have gotten the impression that failure was bad. And you may have started to avoid things you thought you might fail at. This is called "perfectionism," and it can be such a debilitating condition that people with advanced cases of it can't live a normal or happy life.

Failure is an intrinsic part of success. Very few successful people will tell you that what they remember are all the successes. Most of them will remember even more vividly the times they failed.

Why? Because failure is a much better teacher than success. When you fail, you learn about yourself and your goal. You get a chance to retool your approach. You find out what you need to learn in order to succeed.

So if you have perfectionist tendencies, now is the time to give them a good, hard look. On the one hand, it's good to be conscientious and want to get things right. This is the part of yourself that you need to nurture.

But if your perfectionism tells you to avoid situations in which failure is possible, then you're letting it go too far. Once you look hard at almost any opportunity, you'll see that failure is possible. So if you let perfectionism take over, you'll miss out on pretty much every opportunity that comes your way.

Happiness 😊

The Declaration of Independence claimed the right of all people to pursue happiness. The pursuit of happiness is what motivates us to succeed. We pursue goals because we think they'll make us happy.

But I bet you can pretty quickly name some goals that did not make you happy in the least. Remember when I asked you to do a household chore that you hadn't been told to do? Taking out the garbage is probably not anywhere in your personal definition of the pursuit of happiness. How about your least favorite subject that you are required to study? Unless you are planning to live the completely unschooled life, you're probably studying some things that don't make you jump up and down with joy.

But although this book is about goal-setting, it's also intrinsically about maturity. And as you mature, your definition of happiness will change. Little children define happiness by their personal comfort and fulfillment at any given moment. But adults define happiness much differently. They know that achieving their goals, which will make them happy, will probably require some sacrifice and maybe even some suffering.

That's life, kid.

But look on the bright side: Little kids' happiness is totally dependent on other people. If the environment around them isn't making them happy, they don't have the power to change it. Along with the responsibility of maturity, you're also gaining the power to shape your world in a way that helps you achieve your goals—and happiness.

Family values and goals

Your family is different from mine. Your homeschool is different from your friend's homeschool. You are different from your sibling or cousin.

No matter how you look at it, goal-setting is deeply affected by who you are, where you live, your family, and everything that has happened to you.

Sometimes there are clashes between what you think you want, what's available in your community, what your parents want for you, what your friends think is cool, etc. Learning how to negotiate these opposing forces is yet another one of those "maturity" things.

You might notice that a homeschooled friend of yours, for example, is not expected to take any advanced math, whereas your parents expect you to take and excel in math classes. That's not fair!

Well, life isn't fair. It just is.

And the question you always have to ask is, how does what I'm doing relate to my goals?

Chances are, your friend's family believes that she will not need advanced math classes, whereas yours believes you will. There could be many reasons for this:

- You have an aptitude for and interest in math; your friend doesn't
- Your family values higher education; your friend's family values living off the grid and avoiding institutions
- Your family knows that your interest in science, for example, requires you to learn advanced math; your friend is planning to be a preschool teacher and doesn't need it

These are just examples of possible reasons for the conflict. There could be many others.

The way that you work through these conflicts is by finding a way to agree on a path that works for you and for your family, if possible. Occasionally family members develop very different values, and as adults the children drift away from the lifestyle they were raised in. But as a minor, you usually have to find a way to work things out.

Goal-setting with your parent, including them in this process, is the best way to get all perspectives heard. What you say about what you want might surprise them, and who knows, they may surprise you, too!

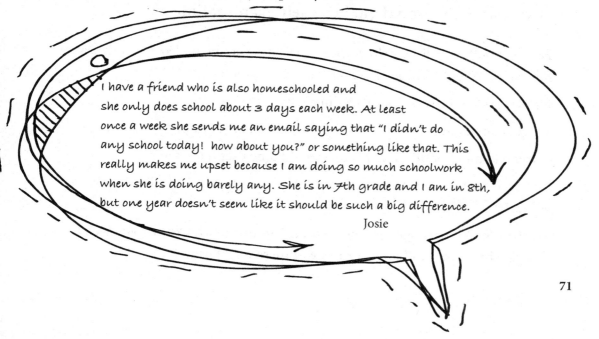

I have a friend who is also homeschooled and she only does school about 3 days each week. At least once a week she sends me an email saying that "I didn't do any school today! how about you?" or something like that. This really makes me upset because I am doing so much schoolwork when she is doing barely any. She is in 7th grade and I am in 8th, but one year doesn't seem like it should be such a big difference.

Josie

Mentorship (Help!)

Before I started homeschooling, I thought "mentorship" was a thing of the distant past. We read biographies of historical figures who, instead of going to college to learn, had a mentor, an older, more skilled person who helped them learn.

Then I started homeschooling, and found out that mentorship is alive and thriving. We don't really focus on it now, but it's a great way for homeschoolers to meet their goals.

In the last section I talked about how parents sometimes have different values than their children. What if you want to be a computer programmer, but your parents are back-to-the-land poets who never studied math?

A mentor is someone who can help you achieve your goals if you find that your parents can't give you the support you need. Usually, parents are quite enthusiastic about helping you find a mentor, because homeschooling parents know that they can't always offer everything you need.

⏩ Exercise 5a: Personal qualities self-examination

For each of the qualities below, reflect in writing, audio, video, or conversation how you see yourself. Use these questions as a guide:

Do you see yourself as having this quality?

What is one example of how you exhibit this quality, or don't exhibit it?

If you had more of this quality, how would it be useful to you?

Can you think of an activity you could do to develop more of this quality in yourself?

If you're working in a group, you could ask someone who knows you well to describe how you exhibit one or more of these qualities well.

1. Flexibility

2. Grit

3. Focus

4. Minimizing bad stress, maximizing good stress

5. Positive use of failure

6. Happiness

▷ Exercise 5b: Defining success for yourself

Brainstorm what you value most in life. Don't censor yourself—if you value having a lot of possessions, then making money is one of your values. I like brainstorming on a large surface—a large piece of paper or a whiteboard. You can also just type all your thoughts into your computer or text chat with a friend, trading ideas.

Write every word that comes to mind when you think about reaching your goals. The thing about brainstorming is that you can just write everything and cross out what you don't like later. (That's why a big sheet of paper might be better than a text chat with a friend.)

Then circle the major items and see if you come up with any themes. For example, if you write "new experiences," "change," and "travel," you might sum those three up by saying that you value a career that doesn't involve going into an office every day. Or if you write "creativity," "using my hands," and "making useful things," you might sum them up by saying that you value a career in industry of some sort.

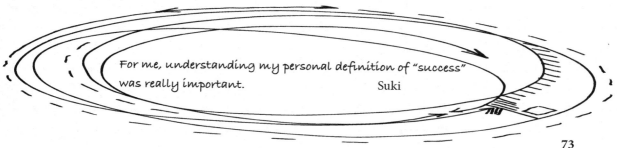

For me, understanding my personal definition of "success" was really important.   Suki

Stretchercize 5: Other people's success

Interview three adults you consider "successful" and ask them for their definition of success. Write down the three definitions. Respond to each from your own point of view, reflecting on why this person's definition does or does not fit your own personal definition. (No need to tell people if you disagree with them! You're doing this for your own personal growth.)

 Recap: In this chapter, we • • •

• • • discussed definitions of "success"
• • • talked about the importance of flexibility, grit, and focus
• • • distinguished good stress from bad stress
• • • identified the importance of failure
• • • tried to figure out what happiness is
• • • discussed how family values affect goals
• • • looked at the importance of mentorship

Onward!

CHAPTER 6

Long-term goal-setting

 Life isn't about finding yourself. Life is about creating yourself.
–George Bernard Shaw

What is "long-term"?

Long-term encompasses everything from "what do I want to complete this year?" to "what am I going to do with the rest of my life?" However, I suggest that you stick a little closer to the present than trying to plan your whole life out. The idea of making long-term goals is *not* to force yourself to stick to them no matter what. That would be very limiting!

The purpose of long-term goals is to give you a general gameplan for the future that you will revise as you grow and change.

What if I don't know what I want to do with my life?

You might have friends who already know what they are going to study in college. People have probably been asking you since you were little what you're going to "be" when you're grown up.

You might find this all a bit distressing.

Don't let it get you down, though. Not everyone knows what they want to do with their lives when they're teens. And I'll tell you a secret: some of the people who think they know what they want will change their minds.

It's not a problem if you don't have a *Master Plan* for your life. You should think of long-term goal-setting as a way to gain experience for the future. For example, you could set a long-term goal of taking one class in each of the academic departments at your community college. Or you could set a goal of pursuing something you find mildly interesting—computer programming, for example, or woodworking—to see where it leads you.

The most important goal you can set for yourself is to be a lifelong learner. Lifelong learners don't feel inhibited by what they have done in the past. They see self-education as an ongoing process, even if they are in a successful career. Lifelong learners don't always feel the need for an overall *Master Plan*.

I know what I'm going to do in ten years— is that OK? ⇐ = = =

Yes, I did just tell your undecided friend above that you might change your mind! But what if that's not the case? What if you already know what your big long-term goal is?

You have been given a gift that others might envy. You can get started as a teen building the foundation you need in order to achieve your goal. That means you may end up achieving your goal early, which is something our culture values.

The thing to remember is keeping a balance: along with grit and focus, you need flexibility. Some people achieve their goals early and then have to find a new goal. Some people think they've achieved their goal but then realize it wasn't what they'd wanted after all.

If you have a *Master Plan* for Life now, that's great. Just make sure that your *Master Plan* is still making you happy along the way.

Learning to live with ourselves: There's a quote I will never forget from the wonderfully nutty 80's movie Buckaroo Banzai: "Wherever you go, there you are." (OK, Confucius said something similar, but it made a big impression on me when it came from Buckaroo!) One of the most important things to learn in life-- almost the definition of "maturity"--is that we have to accept ourselves. We literally can't get away from ourselves. Those of us with diagnosed challenges like ADHD or ASD learn this lesson pretty early. Others might have to work harder.

In my case, when I was young, I thought if I went to live in another country I'd be able to be a different person. So I moved to France, and that's when it hit me: "Wherever I go, there I am." I was in Paris, but I was still me with all my gifts and deficits. Time to get used to being me.

The importance of having long-term goals

Whether you know what you want or not, long-term goals allow us to see meaning in the short-term when things might not look so sunny. If you are struggling with a hard math class, it's worth remembering your long-term goal of becoming an engineer and designing airplane engines. If you are having a conflict with friends or family over your choice to homeschool instead of going to the magnet school that you just got into, you can keep clarity by remembering that homeschooling now suits your long-term goals for yourself.

The importance of celebrating small increments

Imagine you get into a great medical school, and after two years you have the option of taking a Master's degree and dropping out. At the beginning, you are thrilled to be meeting your long-term goal of being a physician. By the second year, however, you've realized you need to go in another direction. That's when you realize how important taking that Master's degree is. You get to celebrate one of the humps that you've made it over in life, even though you decided not to continue to the big prize you had previously wanted.

It's always worth celebrating when you achieve a step in a long-term goal, even if you just give yourself an internal pat on the back. You don't have to throw a party every time you finish a chapter of a book you're writing, but it can feel really great to tell someone about it, check it off a list, or announce it in your writing group.

Failure in meeting long-term goals

We already discussed the value of failure, but usually people see more value in small failures than large ones. Not getting that M.D. after his name may have discouraged our med student who took a Master's instead. He might be tempted to see his entire life as a failure.

But just like when we fail at smaller goals, we are sometimes going to fail at long-term goals, and we have to find some value in it in order to move forward. Maybe our med student met his future wife at med school—how can he regret having tried to meet that goal?

It's all about what we've already discussed, balancing flexibility, grit, and focus so that we don't end up making ourselves miserable.

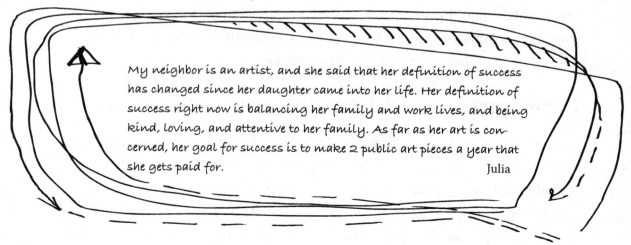

My neighbor is an artist, and she said that her definition of success has changed since her daughter came into her life. Her definition of success right now is balancing her family and work lives, and being kind, loving, and attentive to her family. As far as her art is concerned, her goal for success is to make 2 public art pieces a year that she gets paid for.

Julia

Redefining success

Sometimes as we mature, we find that we redefine success. Our rock musician did that—at first, he really wanted to be a rock star. But once he fell in love with being in the recording studio and started to take pride in his accomplishments, he stopped seeing "rock star" as his definition of success.

I talked earlier about how society attempts to impose its own ideas of success on us. Life is a constant process of remembering to stay true to ourselves. Sometimes we have to shut out a very loud chorus of disapproving voices!

My mom said that the definition of success depends on what you're thinking about or working on, and it changes over time. When she was in school, her definition of success was getting good grades and understanding the subjects. When she got out of school, her definition of success was getting a job and paying loans. She also said "success is when you feel good about what you've done." If you've done a good deed or helped someone, that can be success too. It depends on your priorities. Julia

When to quit and how to be OK about it

"Quitter" is one of the meanest things you can say to someone. We value grit in our society. But is our computer scientist a quitter because she found a slightly different career that she wanted to pursue instead? Is our med student a quitter because he realized the doctoring life wasn't for him?

A quitter is someone who stops trying to reach their goals, not someone who thinks deeply about whether they are on the right path. It's true that if you change goals every time an obstacle comes up, you may quickly form the habit of quitting rather than persevering.

But if you want to quit something, here's the question to ask: Am I quitting because I reevaluated my goal? Or am I quitting because I'm scared I won't make my goal?

If you have reevaluated, then quitting is just an adjustment of your path.

If you are simply scared of failure, then you really are just quitting and you might want to reconsider your options.

When to persevere

No one can ever tell you what the right choice is for sure. All you can do is try to make the most reasoned decision possible and then move forward.

Sometimes you may find yourself in a dreadful position. Maybe you're taking a class with a teacher you really don't like. Maybe you've always found acquiring new ice skating skills easy, but the Double Lutz is doing you in.

The questions you can ask yourself include:

- Is this a necessary step toward reaching my goal?
- Is there some other way I can reach my goal?
- If I need to stay on this path, how can I take a new approach that might be more successful?

This might be a time to look for help from other students, adults in the field, or even just a friend who can offer sound advice.

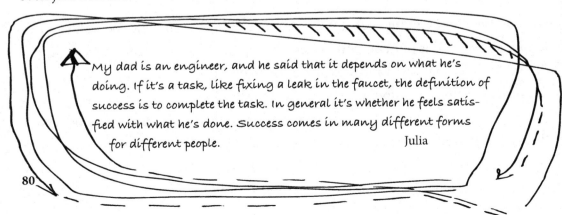

My dad is an engineer, and he said that it depends on what he's doing. If it's a task, like fixing a leak in the faucet, the definition of success is to complete the task. In general it's whether he feels satisfied with what he's done. Success comes in many different forms for different people.

Julia

When other people get in your way

Many of your simpler goals probably depended on two things: your commitment, and the time it took to get the goal done.

Most of our more important goals in life have one very important added factor: other people.

- Maybe you need to get rides to the horse ranch where you want to volunteer because it's not on any bus lines
- Maybe you need to get a good grade from a professor who says he hardly ever gives A's
- Maybe the only violin teacher in your town charges more money than your family can afford
- Maybe there's a student in a class you need who is driving you crazy
- Maybe you have to win an election

When reaching your goal involves other people, you might be tempted to think of them as "getting in your way." If you think this way, though, you are making things unnecessarily hard for yourself, and losing a valuable resource.

Pretty much any goal worth striving for is going to involve other people: teachers, coaches, fellow students, employers—maybe even employees. How you deal with other people is large part of whether you will succeed.

Interpersonal skills

When you have to interact with other people in fulfilling your goal, what you need is "interpersonal skills." Some of us don't learn those easily, especially if we have ADHD or are on the autism spectrum.

It's helpful to take a good look at yourself and how people respond to you:

→ Do people act like you're demanding when you think you're being polite?

→ Do people often misunderstand what you need?

→ Do people ignore you?

The temptation is to think that the problem is with other people. But think about it this way: You can't change other people. You can, however, study up on how you deal with other people and see if you can learn more effective—and less damaging—skills. You may find you end up with more friends, too.

Leadership skills

When you are in a position to influence other people, what you need is "leadership skills." Good leaders don't necessarily act in ways that you might think by watching TV shows or even reading history. There have been many really awful leaders, both in fiction and real life, who succeeded in spite of themselves.

→ Do people always seem to argue with your suggestions?

→ Do people not take your ideas seriously?

→ Are you hesitant to speak up and take leadership when you need to?

Again, you can't change other people. But you can work on your own skills and be the best leader you can be.

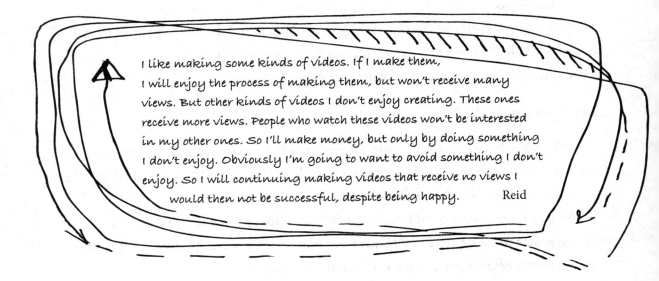

I like making some kinds of videos. If I make them, I will enjoy the process of making them, but won't receive many views. But other kinds of videos I don't enjoy creating. These ones receive more views. People who watch these videos won't be interested in my other ones. So I'll make money, but only by doing something I don't enjoy. Obviously I'm going to want to avoid something I don't enjoy. So I will continuing making videos that receive no views I would then not be successful, despite being happy.   Reid

Setting up a support system

I tell parents who are just starting to homeschool that their #1 task is to set up a homeschool support system.

I'm going to tell you the same thing! (Surprised?)

It's such a temptation to think you can "go it alone." It seems so strong and romantic, doesn't it?

When you were two years old, you probably proudly announced to your parents, "I did it all by myself!"

But now you're a teenager and you need to learn something important: No one does it all by themselves. Everyone who succeeds has some sort of support system. For most people, it's a loose network of family and friends who support them and cheer them on.

But you can set up a support system that works for you, and it doesn't matter what it is so long as it works.

Maybe you have a group of teens who are working through this book together. Maybe you're in a class that will end, but that's no reason to let the support end, right? Make sure to approach other students you work well with before class ends so that you can keep connected with them.

Maybe you've been working with a mentor on something really specific. For example, your mentor is a biologist doing research on local aquatic plant life, and you are entering data for her. Doesn't sound terribly supportive, does it? Well, the only step you need to take in order to add the biologist to your support system is to ask. She might say no. But if you ask something like, "Can I email you about some goals that I'm working on and how I think I'm going to work toward them?" she'll probably say yes.

Maybe you've always worked well with your parent and you want to continue. That's really cool!

Maybe right now you're thinking, "I wish I had a support system!" You need to start at the beginning and build one. That might seem daunting, but it's just like any other goal. Write up your goal, then figure out a few steps you need to take to start on it. Find a way to hold yourself accountable so you don't forget about it. If the first direction you take doesn't work, try a different one.

Your support system should do a few things for you:

- Remind you how cool you are—really: make sure to have people in your life who tell you what's great about you!
- Keep you on track when you want to wander—we all wander sometimes, by the way
- Don't try to force you to do things you think are wrong—some people think that's what "support" is, and they're wrong
- Keep you accountable for what you set out to do—it's easy to get sidetracked

Most people start as teens without much of a support system, and slowly see it grow as they mature. So don't worry if you're starting small. One person who thinks you're cool is enough to start with!

⏩ Exercise 6a: Look to the future

If you know what you want to do for your life's work, research what sort of training and education you will need. Based on that, write a series of smaller goals that you need to attain in order to get there.

If you don't know what you want to do for your life's work, or if you have too many things you want to do, make a long-term goal of exploring a new study or skill each semester. Write down this goal and post it on the wall! You can even make slots with dates so that you write how you achieved this goal each semester. Make sure to set "stretch" goals—things you might feel slightly uncomfortable doing.

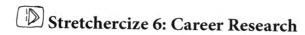 Stretchercize 6: Career Research

Research three people who became successful at what they did. (Remember to use a wide view of "success," not a narrow view.) Try to find three people who were successful in different domains, for example, business, art, and science. Reflect on what they had in common as they worked to attain their goals. Reflect on what they did differently, and why.

Exercise 6b:

Remember that Goal-Setting Questionnaire from Chapter 1? Do you remember where you filed it?

Don't go get it! Not yet, at least. I want you to do it again without reading your original answers. Why? I'll explain after you do it!

So…. go back to the beginning and photocopy it again, or you can download the pretty version at SukiWessling.com/goal/. Please fill it out without looking at your original version. After you fill it out, put the two sets of answers side-by-side and notice the differences. Then you can complete the last activities in this book.

Exercise 6d: Assess yourself

Write, video, draw… However you like to do it, reflect on your answers to the questionnaire. Are they really similar? If yes, what does this say about you (or about this book)? Are they different? If yes, why do you think they are different? Here are some ideas to ponder while looking at the two versions:

- Your feelings about yourself and what you're like may change depending on when you think about them
- Doing the goal-setting activities in this book may have changed the way you look at yourself

- Doing the goal-setting activities in this book may have helped you to be more introspective so you know more about yourself
- Reading this book may have inspired you to try to change something about the way you approach your goals

▷ Exercise 6e: Evaluate this goal-setting approach

What did you think of this book? Did you think it worked well for you as a homeschooler? For someone your age? For someone with your interests? Were the exercises helpful? Did they help you stretch outside of your comfort zone? Would you recommend this book to other homeschoolers you know?

I would love to hear what you think! (I love helpful suggestions, by the way, so feel free to make them.) To get your suggestions to me, you can do one of the following things:

- Email me at teach@SukiWessling.com
- Post your feedback on the book's Amazon.com page—go to SukiWessling. com/goal/ to get the link
- Post your feedback on the book's Goodreads page—go to SukiWessling. com/goal/ to get the link
- Post your feedback on your blog or on your Youtube channel and email me a link

▷ Further reading

Are you interested in reading more about topics in this book? Watching videos where people talk about their own goals and how they achieved them? Visit SukiWessling.com/goal/ for chapter-by-chapter reading and viewing suggestions from the goal-setting class I teach online, plus a list of recommended books for teens.

Recap: In this chapter, we . . .

- • • defined "long-term"
- • • talked about how some people don't know what they want to do
- • • talked about the potential problems with knowing exactly what you want
- • • discussed the importance of having long-term goals
- • • discussed the importance of celebrating small increments
- • • talked about how sometimes we fail to meet long-term goals
- • • discussed changing course and being flexible
- • • redefined success
- • • considered when to quit and how to be OK about it
- • • considered when to persevere
- • • discussed the role of other people in your goals and developing interpersonal and leadership skills
- • • looked at how to set up a support system

Carpe diem!

Afterword

So...have you gotten anywhere?

At the beginning of this book, I wrote that I hoped that this book would help you think more clearly about what you want to get from your homeschool education.

Some of you probably feel like a lightbulb turned on. You were ready to hear what I had to say and you feel more confident. Maybe you've had some great talks with your parent about retooling your homeschooling goals. Maybe you've realized that you were already doing goal-setting, and this book made you aware of it. Maybe you've realized that this is what will help you communicate more clearly with your parent and with teachers.

If so, I'm really glad I could help you. As a friend of mine who speaks Japanese likes to say:

Ganbatte! 頑張って

That means: Go forth and seize the day! You're ready!

Some of you are feeling dismay right now. You went through this book and did the exercises, maybe alone, with a parent, or with a group of students. Maybe you had a good time. Maybe you think I am evil. But you got through it.

And now you're wondering what the fuss was about. You don't feel like you've changed at all. This goal-setting stuff still seems boring and pointless to you. You and your parent may right now be glaring at each other across the dinner table.

In that case, I still hope that your work on goal-setting wasn't lost time. I hope that what's going on is that you're just not quite "there" yet. I've noticed in so many kids over the years that there's something that happens. Educators call it "develop-mental readiness." But you can just call it *"being there."*

- When you're *there*, things make sense to you.
- When you're *there*, you feel like you're in the groove and things are moving smoothly.
- When you're *there*, stuff you heard in the past suddenly comes up in your brain and makes sense to you.

I bet you've been "there" before:

- You practiced and practiced a skill (violin, skateboard, soldering–the tool doesn't matter) and suddenly you're *there*.
- You've tried the same sort of math problem over and over, and it never made sense, then someone explained it a slightly different way and you're *there*.
- You used to hate doing something that your family always does (bike trails, visiting Grandma, eating at that same restaurant), then one day you realize that you like it, too, and you're *there*.

I hope that if you're not *there* with this book right now, you will be in the future. Maybe I've planted a few seeds.

 For all of you

I really do hope that this book was helpful to you.

Do you remember what I said in the beginning of the book? No one ever did this sort of thing for me. I feel like I've spent my life walking backwards into the things that I've ended up wanting to do. It's like I happened upon things and thought, *Well, OK, this is something I enjoy.*

It would have been much easier, and much more fun, if I'd had a sense of where I was going to begin with. Now I do—I'm heading toward the end of this book!

Thank you for spending your time with me. May your future goal-setting be flexible, gritty, focused, productive, and fun!

Ganbatte!

Acknowledgements

This book wouldn't have happened without so many people, I'm sure I will forget to list a few! Thanks to...

→ Kirsten Stein, owner of <u>Athena's Advanced Academy</u>, for her constant support and encouragement and for providing the place where I find my wonderful students

→ My wonderful students, especially my "guinea pigs" who provided me with an active, supportive online community and also the quotations in this book

→ Lilli Wessling Hart, my sister, who reads my work and helps me with book design (thanks for the scribbles!)

→ My parents, Mimi and Rich, who raised five kids and also pursued goals of their own

→ My husband Herb, who proofreads my work, asks me hard questions, and is a great partner who supports all of my crazy schemes (a.k.a. goals)

→ My children, Abe and Chance, who challenged me to become a better person so I could be the best parent possible

→ Extra thanks to Chance for my excellent target logo...

CPSIA information can be obtained
at www.ICGtesting.com
Printed in the USA
FSOW04n0752060917
38254FS